Feeling Outnumbered?

How to Manage and Enjoy Your Multi-Dog Household

SECOND EDITION

Karen B. London, Ph.D.
Patricia B. McConnell, Ph.D.

Cover Design by Julie Mueller, jam graphics
Inside Photo by Alissa Behn

For information, contact:
McConnell Publishing, Ltd.
P.O. Box 447
Black Earth, WI 53515
608/767-2435
www.patriciamcconnell.com

Printed in the United States of America

4 5 6

TABLE OF CONTENTS

A young man was out running with his four American Eskimos when he passed another man pushing his twin daughters in a stroller with two Golden Retrievers walking along side. The two men looked at each other in a moment of mutual admiration and understanding before the father quipped, "I am quite certain that four of a kind beats two pair!"

INTRODUCTION

Those of us who have more than one dog are in a special club of sorts whose members know certain inalienable truths. For example, we know that two dogs are more than twice as much work as one, and that three dogs are as much work as we'd expected seven to be. But we also noticed that the love multiplies faster than the work, and that more really can be merrier. In fact, many of us cannot imagine having only one dog—how empty the house (and the car and the yard and the heart) would be.

This booklet is about maximizing the joys of living with more than one dog. It offers specific, practical ideas to help you enjoy your dogs even more. Whether you are looking for some tips for creating a bit of order out of the canine chaos in your home, or trying to manage tension between two or more dogs, this booklet can help. Some sections in this booklet deserve to be books all by themselves, and we encourage you to read elsewhere in more depth about any issue that seems especially important to your situation. (Check the recommendations at the end of this booklet.) Think of this booklet as a concise and basic guide book— the "Cliff Notes" to multi-dog-dom.

Our approach to managing multi-dog households departs from the old advice of determining which dog is alpha and supporting that dog's position by feeding first, petting first, and so on. Instead, we teach all of our dogs to be polite, patient, and respectful, and we tolerate no fighting or "working it out." We teach specific activities to groups of dogs to encourage harmony in multi-dog households.

The viewpoints and techniques we describe have helped many of our clients, and we hope they will help you as well, no matter what's going on in your pack. Many of us just need to tone down the chaos that ensues when several dogs greet visitors. Others may need to manage escalating tension between two or three dogs. (Keep in mind, however, that if your dogs are at risk of being seriously aggressive with each other, we urge you to consult a qualified dog trainer or behaviorist. No small booklet can treat a potentially life-threatening problem and it is best to get professional help in both evaluating the situation and in treating it.)

Many multi-dog problems do not involve serious aggression, but are about dogs who are unruly and just need to learn to be more polite. So often, the pushiest dogs get what they want, and they get it first and fastest. This situation promotes a society in which each individual has everything to gain by being pushy and everything to lose by being patient. If your dogs learn that they can "win" in life by being pushy and competitive, then you will have dogs who may not be much fun to be around. On the other hand, if your dogs learn that being patient and polite leads to toys, food and fun, then life at your house will most likely become much more pleasant. In some cases this strategy can help avoid the potential of serious aggression problems between dogs in your home.

This booklet focuses on teaching your dogs to be polite and patient rather than pushy and demanding. The ideas and real life strategies are not meant to be an instant cure for all troubles, but are offered to help you and your dogs have more fun living together in one house.

LAYING A FOUNDATION

Work With Each Dog Individually

Spending one-on-one time with each of your dogs is an important factor in helping them pay attention to you when they're in a group. This may seem obvious, but it's easy to forget when you're caught up in a sea of swirling tails and thundering paws. It never hurts to remind ourselves that if our dogs fail to establish a private relationship with us, then their primary relationships will be with the other dogs in the house. After all, dogs inherently speak "dog," not English, and dogs are surely much easier for other dogs to understand and communicate with than a human—even one who loves them as much as you do. When communicating with your dogs, it's helpful to remember that you speak their language with a pretty thick accent and that it takes a lot of effort for your dogs to understand you. Quality time spent with each dog goes a long way towards your dog feeling connected to you and being willing to do what you want. As much as you love your big, crowded pack, some of your most cherished moments with your dogs might happen when you're one-on-one.

Work with each dog individually whenever you are teaching one of your dogs a new behavior. It is too distracting for you and your dog to have other dogs around when you're both trying to concentrate. Training demands complete focus so that your signals and timing are precise. It is too hard to give one hundred percent of your focus to your "student dog" when you have another dog in the mix. Don't set yourself up to fail by trying to teach something new in a situation that is too distracting, as it surely is with another dog around. So have your other dogs in a different room, out in the yard if that is safe for them, in the car if it's not too warm, out on a walk with a spouse or roommate— any place safe, but away from you and the dog you are training.

Once your dog can do the new behavior without distractions, begin to work on it with another dog present. Again, set your dog up to succeed, which means that your expectations for the behavior will take into account that it is much harder to do with other dogs around. For example, if you have worked up to a 45-second stay with no distractions, you might ask for a five-second stay with another dog present. When you first have the other dog around, put her behind a gate, on leash with another person, or on a stay (if she can reliably hold one) while you work with your student dog. Add additional dogs one at a time and only gradually have the other dogs be more active during training sessions. Perhaps this advice seems simplistic, but just because something is simple doesn't mean that it's easy! When you have several dogs, you will be swimming upstream to spend time with each of them individually, but it's worth it in the long run. After all, if your dog won't listen to you when the two of you are alone, you can't expect to gain her attention when the whole group is around.

Master the Important Commands

Whether you have two dogs or an even dozen of them, solid obedience training is a fundamental part of a happy, multi-dog household. All of your dogs need to learn what behavior is appropriate and what behavior is unacceptable. Perhaps the most important piece of this is that each dog needs to know that it is in her best interest to do what you request. Work toward training in which there is clear communication between you and your dogs, and training in which the dog has everything to gain by doing what you ask, and nothing to gain by ignoring you. To control a pack that tends toward the "exuberantly unruly," it helps to have all of your dogs know their own name, and a phrase such as "wrong" or "no" that is not so much a "correction," but rather an instruction to stop what they are doing. Additionally, you will never regret working to get all of your dogs rock solid as individuals on just a few

4

basic commands—come, sit or down, and stay. We encourage you to get a training manual that is rooted in an understanding of dog behavior and that emphasizes positive training methods. Whether you use clicker training, a marker word like "yes" or "good," lure and reward training or any other fun, upbeat method, learn to use positive reinforcement to train your dogs. (Again, check out some of our favorite books at the end of the booklet.)

Oh, is that all, you ask? Did I just buy this booklet only to be told that if I train my dogs, they will be better trained? But, bear with us here. We know that you are aware that training your dog has big pay-offs, and that training is time well spent. However, part of effective dog training is choosing what to emphasize in your training efforts, and this booklet suggests what to prioritize. For training to be as beneficial as possible, you need to work with your dogs enough that they *master* a few basic commands. Knowing a large number of commands can be valuable, but if your dogs have mastered just a few commands, you will be able to handle and enjoy just about any situation life throws your way.

There is a big difference between simply *knowing* a command and truly *mastering* it. For example, many tennis players "know" how to hit a perfect serve, but not all can do it when they're distracted or nervous and the crowd is cheering for the other guy. You need your dogs to do what you ask when they are barking hysterically at the door, not just when you are by yourselves with no distractions. Similarly, it is a lovely start to have your dog come when called when alone in the backyard. But, if another dog invites your dog to play, will she come then?

To master a command, you must work on it until the response becomes automatic for both you and your dog. You get that through practice, practice, practice. The good news is that you don't need to practice for very long. Just a few short training sessions every day, even for as little as five or fifteen seconds, can be extremely useful.

Repetition can be important when first training a dog, so you want to ask your dog to do something four to five times in early training sessions. But once she's gotten the idea, asking just once or twice in a row, several times during the day is great practice. Be sure not to overdo repetitions, as too much can bore or confuse your dog.

Your dogs will learn best and enjoy the process more if you know exactly what it is that they are willing to work for. Your challenge is to figure out what your dogs' passions really are. Many dogs are motivated by food, especially if it's the good stuff—cheese, chicken, steak or cooked carrots—rather than the less exciting dry biscuit. Other dogs will do anything for tennis balls, squeaky toys, a belly rub, a bone, or a good old-fashioned game of chase. For best results, mix and match the reinforcements so your dog learns that he feels good when he does as you ask, but also gets surprised by exactly how. Keep 'em guessing!

After many short practice sessions at a low level of distraction, gradually increase the distraction level. Don't jump from a sit-stay in the kitchen with just one dog to a sit-stay at the dog park with the whole group. There are at least 50 steps between the first lessons of a command like "come," and actually using that command in the chaos of life. Each step represents an increasing level of difficulty for your dogs. Coming in the house when they hear the treat bag rattle might be step 3, but coming to you away from a pack of dogs playing ball might be step 48. Great trainers are always mindful of how difficult it is for their dogs to comply, and carefully structure their training so that their dogs are never asked to do something too far above their ability. After all, would you expect musicians to play well at Carnegie Hall if they'd never performed in public before? All trainers know the importance of "proofing" dogs at increasing levels of distraction for a competition or performance, but somehow it's not intuitively obvious how much proofing is also needed at home. Since everyday life in a multi-dog household is inherently filled with distractions for each of your dogs, proofing is particularly important. The key is to make sure your dog *can* comply and is *glad* when he does.

Teach A Group Name

If you have lots of dogs, it's helpful to be able to get all of your dogs' attention at once. Teach all of your dogs a group name such as "dogs" or "shepherds" or use the term "goof balls" or "bozos" if you want to (yet another reason why having lots of dogs can be fun!). Teach each dog to pay attention when you say "dogs" by saying it and then giving a treat to every dog who looks at you. Having a group designation for all your dogs is just as handy as it is to call your children for dinner by saying, "Kids, dinnertime!" rather than "Brian..., Evan..., Taylor..., Dinnertime!" You might even find it helpful to have group names for different categories of your dogs. You can decide what subcategories will be helpful in your household, but don't underestimate your dogs' abilities to understand group names.

Life Is Not Always Fair and That's Okay

We all want to be kind and loving to all of our dogs and give them a wonderful life. Some people think that this means treating all of our dogs the same, every moment, in an effort to be fair. For example, if one dog gets a pill wrapped in cheese, this line of thinking would lead to giving every dog a treat. But if dogs never see another dog with something they can't have, they can become intolerant of being denied anything. Giving your dogs what they want all the time does not necessarily make them happy. What they want in the short term is not always what is best for them in the long term, so love your dogs enough to resist giving in to them every time they look at you longingly.

It may seem counterintuitive, but one way to create a harmonious household is to give up on the idea of equality. There are at least two reasons for this. First, trying to treat all of your dogs the same every moment, besides being an impossible goal, interferes with your ability to treat each of your dogs as individuals. As individuals, all of your dogs have different needs for attention, exercise, food, training, play, and the type of rules that they must follow to be upstanding citizens. Besides, your dogs don't expect life to be fair all the time. That idea is not part of their natural history—dogs are comfortable with the idea of differences. Second, and perhaps most important, dogs, like humans, need to learn to cope with the frustration of not getting everything they want every time they want it. It's just part of the reality of life, and we all, dogs included, need to learn to cope with it.

Dogs are capable of throwing the same kinds of tantrums that small children (and some adults!) exhibit, except that instead of kicking and screaming and turning red, these dogs often take their problems out on another dog close by. So, do your dogs a favor, teach them to be patient and flexible, and give yourself permission to treat each one differently when you need to.

If two of your dogs can handle having free rein in the house, but your third likes to remodel walls and furniture, is it reasonable to crate the remodeler and not the others? Of course! If one of your dogs dominates the Frisbee® so that the other dogs never get to play, is it okay to play Frisbee® with one of the others alone? Sure! If going on a long Sunday run with one of your dogs is your idea of heaven, but going on that same run with two or three of them is a nightmare, take one and leave the others behind. It's okay!

If one of your dogs gets to sleep on the bed and this has no ill effects on behavior, but your other dogs get an exaggerated sense of their own importance if allowed to do the same, does everybody have to stay on the floor? Not necessarily. The bed issue arises frequently during private consultations and tends to be a loaded issue. Whether being on the bed is okay or not is difficult to determine because it varies so much from dog to dog and family to family. There are families where it works out just fine to have some dogs on the bed and some restricted to the floor. Make this decision based on your individual dogs, not out of a sense that all dogs have to be treated the same, or that it's wrong to let some dogs sleep on the bed.

Status

Sometimes part of the trouble that occurs between family dogs is the result of confusion in the social order. However, labeling a problem as "status-related" (the term dominance is commonly used, though not often correctly) is perhaps the most common misdiagnosis of dog behavior. Many dog owners believe or have been told that their dogs have a "dominance" problem when this is not the case. Nonetheless, status-related problems do occur, and the fact that this problem is over-diagnosed is no reason to eliminate the concept entirely. Conflict between members of social groups, even ones made up of different species, is inevitable. One way in which conflict is handled without aggression is to have a very clear social order in which the relative status of members is clear to everyone in the group.

However, hierarchical social structures don't simply consist of the "dominant" individual and "the rest of the pack." The structure is more complex. Most aggression in social groups of species like humans and dogs seems to be in "middle management," or from the high-ranking members who may not be dominant, but who have first access to the CEO. Keeping dogs from assuming this status category seems to help eliminate group tension and aggression. For example, if three of your dogs perceive themselves as in a competition for positions 2, 3, and 4 in the hierarchy, then there's a lot to compete for. After all, the silver medal is a lot better than the bronze at the Olympics. But if your dogs learn that social status isn't the key to getting what they want—while being patient and polite is—they will be less likely to throw their weight around to get what they want.

You can also help prevent status-related aggression by being a calm and confident leader, projecting a sense of benevolent power. You can do that by setting boundaries for your dogs without intimidating them, and by loving them without spoiling them. If your dogs learn that they can "win" in life with pushy, obnoxious, competitive behavior, then you will have a family of rude dogs who may not be much fun. On the other hand, if your dogs learn that being polite and patient leads to access to toys and food and fun and games and love, then life at your house will most likely be closer to what you had in mind. You can promote a society in which every individual benefits by being polite, and loses by being pushy.

So, don't let your dogs act like spoiled princes and princesses, getting everything they want by some canine equivalent of stomping their feet. You can be loving and benevolent and still be the one who decides when it's dinnertime, when it's play time, and when your dogs get petted. If your dog runs into you while going out the door, gets your attention every single time he demands it, and is the one who decides when to play, why would he listen to you when he's about to start something with the new dog you just brought home?

To control pushy behavior, teach the lessons of patience and tolerance advocated in this booklet, like group "offs" and group "waits." Granted, these lessons are easier for some dogs to learn than for others. To some dogs, patience and politeness come very naturally, but for others it can be much more of a struggle, just like controlling one's temper is easy for some people and a lifelong struggle for others. Some dogs are able to handle frustration better than others, and some are just naturally happy to wait their turn. Thus, it is crucial that you work with each dog as an individual and are prepared to work extra hard with the dogs that find these life lessons just a little more difficult. Every dog teaches us something special, and one of your dogs may be the one who is teaching *you* to be patient. Ironic, isn't it?

GETTING PRACTICAL:
SPECIFICS FOR REAL LIFE

Body Blocks

Controlling the behavior of your dogs without having to touch them is a goal worth time and effort. If you rely on a leash and collar or a truly "hands-on" approach to training, you will never have the "anytime, anywhere" control over your dogs that we all want, and that we all need if we have a lot of dogs. Some dogs treat the leash as the cue to mind their owners but are oblivious to signals to sit, stay, or come when the leash is out of the picture. But dogs often exert tremendous control and influence over the behavior of other dogs, all without leashes, collars, or grabbing for each other. How do *they* do it?

An influential dog controls other dogs' movements by managing the space around them. She puts her body in front of another dog, blocking the way that she does not want him to go, and leaving him access to the way that she does want him to go. She is communicating to him, "Not this way, try another route." Herding dogs are particularly adept at this space management and use it on other animals in addition to dogs. Working Border Collies move animals all the time without touching them, and they do it by taking charge of space. In a similar way, soccer goalies, in their attempts to keep the ball out of their own goal, do so by protecting the space around the goal rather than by trying to directly control the behavior of the ball.

If one dog uses her body to control space but another dog keeps coming, a confident dog will hold her ground. It's not that she's going out of her way to collide with the other dog, she's just committed to controlling that space. You can use the same principles to influence the behavior of your dog without grabbing at him. To do that, focus on using your legs and torso rather than your hands—it is more understandable to your dog. Dogs don't use their paws to control each other, they use their whole body.

11

For maximum effectiveness, follow their example and use your torso, not your "paws" if you need to make contact to influence your dogs' behavior. Do it their way, taking a "When in Rome, do as the Romans do" approach and you'll be amazed at what you can accomplish. With a few adjustments to allow for human anatomy (particularly that two-legged thing), the blocking motions of dogs can be translated into a suite of behaviors that you can use to control your dogs by managing the space around them.

We call these space management maneuvers "body blocks" and we use them in a variety of contexts. Using body blocks effectively requires that you attend to both your body's position in space and its movements, including side-to-side movements as well as whether you are moving forward or backward relative to your dog. Body blocks are easier to demonstrate in person, but you can get the idea from the following descriptions of how to move your body when doing body blocks in specific contexts.

Say you've put your dog on a stay, and she starts to get up and investigate the cornbread crumbs that you've dropped behind you on the kitchen floor. If she moves forward toward you and to your left, counter her with your own forward motion, stepping forward and sideways just one step into the space that she was about to occupy. You've just done a body block. With many dogs, just blocking the space that your dog was about to occupy is enough to stop them from proceeding. If she does pause, then you should respond by leaning or moving back yourself, taking the pressure off her, but ready to move right or left again if she initiates another break. Exactly how assertive you need to be in occupying the space depends on your dog. Some sensitive dogs will stop and back up if you just lean toward them. But some dogs are oblivious to a mere lean, and require much more movement on your part in order to concede the space. For any dog, the sooner you react the better. Once you and your dog are both experienced, you can simply lean forward an inch or two just as your dog starts the first shift of weight to move off of her stay. Some physically pushy dogs will ignore you at first and just keep right on coming. Stay silent, but "talk" with your body by continuing to block the space that your dog is trying to occupy. Be ready to shift right or left like a soccer goalie, putting your feet and legs in her way, until she stops trying to get past you and looks up at you. The microsecond she settles back into her stay, reward her by giving her a tasty treat.

Besides teaching a solid stay, you can use body blocks to keep uninvited dogs from jumping into your lap, leaping onto your chest or dancing on your head, as some overly friendly nine-ty-pound dogs often try to do when you're sitting on the couch. Remember that dogs don't use their paws to push other dogs away, so don't try to push demanding dogs away with your hands. Rather, keep your hands tucked into your chest, lean forward with your torso and push the dog away with your body, just like dogs do. Again, adjust your body block to the sensitivity of your dog. Try it the next time some overly enthusiastic dog begins a charge for your lap. Long before they get to you, tuck your hands across your torso, and lean forward to block the dog with your shoulder, hip or elbow, sitting right back up after the dog has moved backward. Most dogs won't give up right away, they'll try again a few times. After all, they've probably been well rewarded for crawling up into someone's lap, even if it's just with attention. The key is to occupy the space before they do, just like a dog who blocks another dog from getting to you by inserting his body between you and that other dog.

In summary, body blocks can take a variety of forms: leaning while standing or seated, shuffling towards your dog, goalie-like behavior which often involves side-to-side movements, and stepping into your dog's direction of movement. What all of these maneuvers have in common is that they allow you to control your dog's move-ment and behavior by managing the space around him. Dogs respond very well to this space management, presumably because it's so natural to them. Many dogs act like a light bulb has gone off in their minds when they are first exposed to humans using body blocks. Perhaps they feel as though their humans are finally making sense. Of course, they can learn to understand humans, just like many of us can learn another language. But oh the joy of traveling in a foreign country and hearing your own language!

In addition to making sense to dogs and therefore being effective, body blocks have some other advantages. You can use body blocks anytime, anywhere. The only required equipment is your own body, which you probably have with you at all times, even on the most hectic of days. No leashes, no collars, no supplies of any kind are necessary. Besides being available to you always, body blocks prevent having dogs who only respond when both of you are attached to a leash. Furthermore, your dogs won't avoid your outstretched hand, as many dogs who have been trained with other methods often do.

Since body blocks are useful in so many different contexts, they will come up repeatedly throughout this booklet. Put body blocks in the category of things to *master*, and you'll find your training skills greatly enhanced.

When Someone Else is the Belle of the Ball

One of the many situations that a dog in a multi-dog household must learn how to handle is watching another dog getting attention or treats. A great way to get your dogs to accept this fact of life is to reinforce one dog for staying in place while you pay attention to another dog. Teach each dog that good things happen if they hold a stay while another dog gets attention. Start this once your dogs already have reliable stays on their own. Then tell one dog to stay beside or behind you. Give a couple of seconds of attention and petting (no more!) to your other dog, who is a couple of steps away from the dog who is on a stay.

Then turn to the dog on a stay, quietly praise and give him a great treat, and then release him from the stay. Do this two to three times in a session. If the dog breaks the stay, body block him back into the stay. If a dog breaks repeatedly, make the task easier for him by practicing his stays in a less distracting setting, or by waiting less time before giving him the treat.

After one or two sessions of this, try this variation. When you turn back to the dog who is on stay, praise and give a treat, but do not release from the stay. Instead, return your attention to the other dog for a couple of seconds, while the sitting dog remains in a stay. Then, turn to the dog in the stay, praise, give a treat, and then release. After about a week of practicing this two to three times a day, increase the amount of time that you expect your dog to stay while you go back and forth between the dogs. The idea is that the dog learns that it's fun to watch you give another dog attention, because it means that good things are about to happen.

Being Comfortable Alone

All dogs should be able to amuse themselves either in a crate or in a room closed off from the household activities. To be able to work with your dogs individually, you must have a place to put the other dogs while you do so. The place can be a crate, a laundry room, a bedroom, or an outdoor kennel. To condition your dog to a confined area of any kind, play a game by having your dog go in and out of the area three to five times in a row to get treats that you have tossed into it. Your dog will begin to learn that the confined area is a fun place to go because when he gets there, something good happens. Play this game every evening for a few days, making sure to let your dog go in and out without shutting the door. Once your dog consistently goes into the area, start to swing the door shut for a single second after he enters and then open it as he finishes eating the treats. After a few more sessions of that, toss in a Kong® or Goodie Ball® stuffed with something delicious, shut the door, and while it is shut, let him spend a few seconds eating the yummy treats out of the toy. Now you have a dog who willingly goes into a confined area and continues to have a good time even when the door is closed.

After a week or so of several sessions a day, begin to leave your dog for longer periods in the area with a stuffed Kong® or Planet Dog's Orbo's® to keep him busy, making sure to use treats that he really wants. Once your dog is really invested in getting the treat, walk away for thirty seconds. Come back *before* he's done eating, open the door, and take the toy away from him. By doing this you are teaching your dog that he gets his special toy only when you leave. He will begin to wonder when you are going to confine him again so he can get back to munching.

Gradually increase the amount of time that your dog is left alone in the confined area, choosing times when your dog is relaxed and most likely to nap. Spend the most time on the earliest stages when you're gone for only short intervals. Once your dog can stay for 30 seconds, one minute, and then five minutes, you can increase the interval more quickly to 30 minutes, one hour, and then two hours.

Use the same area for all of your dogs, or use different ones, based on what works best for both you and your dogs. If your dogs are happier being confined together, work with pairs of dogs. You may need to provide extra goodies so that there is more than enough to go around. If your dogs could be aggressive over food, or for some other reason are better off being confined as individuals, condition each of them to their own crates or to a different area of your house.

No matter what's going on at your house, being able to confine your dogs is a handy trick to have. We all have to deal with events like visiting relatives who don't like dogs, the disruption of installing a new kitchen floor, or a back door that has blown off its hinges. (You are correct if you perceive the voice of experience here in these real life examples.)

Dinnertime Manners

For many dogs, the dinner hour is THE event of the day. Heck, for many people (including us) it is, too! Snoopy even had his special suppertime dance to celebrate the joy of it. But in households with large packs of dogs, dinnertime can be just a little *too* exciting. One of the things that makes feeding time extra interesting in multi-dog households is the issue of who gets what. Many dogs seem to feel as though the kibble is always tastier on the other side of the bowl, taking a "what's mine is mine, what's yours is mine" approach to meals. Other dogs are concerned with hurrying up and eating before another dog comes over to see what they've got.

There are a couple of ways to make dinnertime a more relaxing experience for everyone. If dinnertime is so chaotic that your dogs cannot safely or comfortably enjoy a meal in the same room, then by all means feed them separately. Put them into different rooms, feed them in their crates, or give each one a nice spot in the house in which to enjoy dinner. If, on the other hand, they are safe eating in the same room, but you feel as though one or more of the dogs is just a little too quick to "bowl-hop," try giving your dogs "dessert."

By giving your dogs dessert, we mean giving them an extra special treat for an alternative behavior—for doing something other than harassing your other dogs. Teach all of your dogs, for example, to go to some other part of the house after they are done eating, rather than trick-or-treating at the other dogs' bowls. You could teach your dogs that if they go to the back door after eating, they'll get something better than the regular food that is still in other bowls. In other words, the way to get dessert is not to go get it from another dog, but to go to another place where it will be served to them.

To teach each dog to look for dessert someplace appropriate, position yourself near the dog that you expect to finish dinner first. When she is done, lure her with a treat toward the back door (or wherever) and away from other dogs' bowls. Use body blocks to prevent her from raiding another dog's dinner. Stay silent if you can to keep the process nice and calm. Once you get your dog to the "dessert area," deliver the tasty morsels right away so that she'll be glad she went there. Because dogs often finish their dinners at different times, you well might be able to do this alone. If you are lucky enough to have several people in your house who'd love to be involved, have each person be in charge of one dog. If you need help, but are short of people relative to dogs, use gates or barriers to prevent your dogs from making a mistake and going to each other's bowls while they are still learning about where to get dessert. Do this over and over every night at dinnertime, until your dogs learn that heading to the dessert bar is a really good idea.

Rather than have your dogs go to another place after dinner to get dessert, an alternative is teaching them to stay by their food bowls when they have finished dinner. You can easily do this by delivering a tasty treat to their bowls just seconds after they finish eating. Gradually wait a little longer each time before delivering a treat to their bowl, until they all stay by their own bowls, waiting for the goodies to come.

Greeting Visitors

Though we love dogs more than we love chocolate, even we aren't crazy about being greeted at the door by the canine equivalent of a Mack truck. Assuming most visitors feel the same, you will be more popular if you teach your dogs a more polite way of behaving at the front door. This is good not just for your human friends, but also good for your dogs. Many dog-dog aggression cases involve dogs who started fighting in the frenzy of greeting visitors at the door. In some ways, the solution to the problem of greeting visitors is simple. Just decide what you would like your dogs to do when people come over, and then teach them to do it. Okay, okay, this sounds foolishly simple, but it's a step that many of us seem to skip. For some reason we train and proof our dogs endlessly for the obedience ring or agility trials, but not at the front door.

Four possible approaches are (1) teach your dogs to back up ten feet or so away from the door before you open it, (2) teach your dogs to sit and stay in a particular spot when people come over, (3) teach them to run and get a toy to redirect their exuberance away from the visitors, or (4) take advantage of your dogs' ability to be comfortable separated from household activities and put them in crates or another room before you let the visitors in. All four approaches keep your dogs from competing for the visitors' attention and make your visitors welcome, rather than encouraging them to make a run for it. For better behaved dogs when visitors arrive, teach your dogs to do the chosen behavior when the doorbell rings or there's a knock at the door. Have a friend or family member ring the bell, then ask your dogs to do what you want them to. After many repetitions, and lots of positive reinforcement, your dogs will respond to the bell or knock with the behavior you have trained them to do.

You can teach your dogs to stop crowding around the door with body blocks and treats, using your body to back them away from the door and then giving them a reinforcement when they're in the area that you'd like. In this case, you haven't necessarily put your dogs on a sit-stay, but they're not allowed to crowd toward the door and your visitors. This approach takes the least training, and once you're comfortable doing body blocks, it often solves the problem pretty quickly. The key is to remember to (1) back your dogs away from the door just by walking quietly toward them until they back up, (2) use your body like a goalie to keep your dogs back where you want them to be, and (3) give your dogs lots of reinforcement for staying in that general area. Start by working with each dog individually, blocking him away from the door to a designated waiting area where he'll get reinforced. Then add a visitor who will stay by the door as you body block your dog into the spot where he will get reinforced. Your choice of reinforcements can make all the difference. If you're going to successfully compete with the excitement of visitors, be armed with the equivalent of filet mignon, rather than wheat germ. Once you have trained all of your dogs individually, work in pairs and then in threesomes. Set it up so your dog-loving friends are your visitors. It's better to practice when you're focused and relaxed, rather than when your boss is coming over for dinner.

Teaching a sit-stay for visitors is much the same. You simply add on a sit and stay command while helpful friends pretend to be "visitors" over and over again. (You can start with your own family going in and out just to get the pattern started.) Be sure to place the dogs at least 8-10 feet away from the door.

Teaching a dog to get a toy works beautifully if you have any dogs who are nuts about toys. Just like some five-year-old kids like to show you their new toys, some dogs can't resist going to get their best toy when they greet visitors. These dogs are easy to teach. Direct them toward their favorite toy whenever you or anyone else enters. A lot of ball-crazy dogs already know a phrase such as "go get your ball," and if you say this each time visitors arrive, and then play with your dogs, they will quickly get the idea that visitors mean playtime. Be sure that you reinforce her when she brings you her favorite toy. If you take the toy away you may be punishing your dog, but if you start a short game of fetch, your dog is more likely to bring it to you the next time you have visitors over.

The Group Wait

Why Teach a Group Wait? If your dog runs into other dogs in her rush to get out the door, she is not being respectful or polite. By teaching your dogs to "wait" at the door and to go out only when you release them one by one, you are taking control of the doorway and rewarding patience and polite behavior. It's truly worth the effort. No longer will your dogs knock you or others over when you open the door. And given that many dog fights occur at doorways, this kind of control is an excellent way of preventing trouble. You don't necessarily need to do this every time your dogs go outside, just often enough that they learn their manners.

Teaching Wait to Individual Dogs Before teaching a group "wait," all of your dogs must be able to "wait" alone, so first work with each dog separately. Face your dog with your body between her and the door so that you can use your body to control her. Have your dog on leash if necessary for safety's sake, but leave the leash loose. (Actually, it works best to have someone else hold the leash, or tie it to a railing, so that you can rely on your body and not the leash.) When your dog approaches the door, walk toward her, herding her away from it. If she tries to dart around you, move quickly to block her with your body. You will feel a bit like a hockey goalie if you are doing this correctly. Once you have moved her back about four feet from the door, say "wait" in a low, even-toned voice, and then partially open the door. Most dogs jump forward when they see the door open, so be ready to block her path to the door with your body if she tries to bolt through.

What you do next depends upon your dog's behavior. If your dog tries to bolt through the door before you have given her permission, block her path with your body or close the door before she can get through it. (Be sure not to slam the door on your dog!) Then shuffle her backward again to a couple of feet from the door. Next, give her another opportunity to be right or wrong by opening the door and stepping out of her way again. (Resist the urge to drape yourself over the entire doorway!) Stand to the side so that she can choose for herself what to do—to wait or to make a break for it. If she chooses to wait, step through the doorway first and then release her by saying her name in a lilting, singsong tone of voice. If her name is only one syllable, it can help to say her name twice, rising in pitch for the second repetition. If her name is more than one syllable, have your voice rise in pitch after the first syllable of her name. She only gets to proceed through the doorway when she stops trying to charge through it. Getting to go outside is her reward for waiting, so there is no need to give her a treat. The great outdoors is the biggest "treat" there is for most dogs.

Repeat the exercise no more than three or four times each session, being sure to end each session on a good note. Note that "wait" is different than "stay." "Stay" means to remain in one place until being released, while "wait" means that your dog can't move forward until released. If you say "wait" and your dog turns away from the door entirely, that is absolutely fine. All you want from a "wait" is for your dog to stop trying to barge through the door; she doesn't need to be on a stay. Look for your dog to hesitate or back away from the door just to the word "wait" itself, without you having to body block her. Once she'll do that consistently, you're ready for the next step.

Teaching Wait with More Than One Dog Once all of your dogs are waiting reliable by themselves, it is time to work on a group "wait." Beware of doing group "waits" without help if you've ever had trouble with serious aggression at the door, but it is one of many tools you can use to prevent it. Begin with two dogs, even if you have three or more at home. Say to your dogs, "Dogs, wait" in a low, no-nonsense tone of voice. There is no need to sound mean or harsh, just be sure that your voice tone is low and doesn't rise in pitch as if asking a question. Keep in mind that this is a new context for them, so they won't necessarily act as they do when there's no other dog there. Even if they don't pressure you to get out the door when alone, they may forget themselves and try to barge out to beat their buddy through the door. Be ready to body block any forward motion like you did before. The instant that both dogs are politely waiting, say one of their names in a lilting voice to release that dog. It's best to release the dog farthest away from you, so you can block the other dog if necessary. Only the dog whose name was called is permitted to come forward and go out the door. Be prepared to body block the other dog—she may hear your "release" tone of voice and be confused, or she may see the other dog moving toward the door and want to get there first. Once the second dog is waiting politely, say her name in a singsong tone of voice and let her go out the door. Repeat this right away in reverse, letting the second dog go through the door first so each dog is reinforced for waiting.

It doesn't take long for most dogs to catch on to this new game. Dogs usually know their own names as well as the names of all the others in the house. Do NOT use "okay" or any other general release word in a group "wait," even if you say a dog's name first. One of us tried very hard to get her dogs to understand that "Spot, okay," just referred to Spot, but to no avail. Once the dogs heard "okay" they all started moving, and were clearly puzzled to be on the receiving end of a body block after hearing "okay" said so clearly.

Refining Your Dogs' Patience in a Group Wait When you practice group "waits," it's important to change the order of who gets to go out the door first. Mix and match so that the dogs never know who gets to go next. One way to decide who gets to go first is by saying the name of the dog who does the best "wait." Hopefully, the next time around, a different dog will do best. But even if one dog is always more patient than the other, be sure to vary who gets to go when.

A Group Wait with the Whole Group Once you have worked with each possible pair of dogs in your household, begin trying it with all the possible threesomes. Say, "Dogs, wait," and wait until all dogs are deferring to you by not putting any pressure on you for access to the door. You may have to go back to your body blocks to achieve this. Then, release one dog by saying his name in that cheerful tone. Be prepared to body block the other two dogs. Then release the second dog by name and be ready to block the remaining dog. Finally, release the last dog by name to go out the door.

Gradually increase the number of dogs waiting at the door until your whole brood is doing a lovely group wait. Ah, the beauty of it! This may sound like a lot of work, but once you start you will find it easier to do than you might think. A group "wait" is not something you have to do every time you go outside, although you will want to use it regularly to keep your dogs' manners in tune.

The Group Off

Did your hamburger fall off the counter? No problem! If you and your dogs have mastered a group "off," simply say "Dogs, off," and the four-footed seas will part and then you can release one of your dogs by name to get it, or pick it up yourself. If your dogs are not already aggressive over food, the "off" command can be very useful in preventing potential problems within any group of dogs. They'll learn that they get what they want by being patient and polite, rather than pushy and assertive. This is much easier to teach to dogs than you might think (honest!), and it is so practical.

Teaching Off to Individual Dogs The signal "off" means to back away from something. Many people use "leave it" to mean the same thing, and either is fine as long as you pick one and stick with it. Before you can do a group "off," all of your dogs must be able to do an "off" by themselves. Start with two treats, one in each hand—one "low value" treat (perhaps an inexpensive small dog biscuit) and a "high value" treat like a piece of chicken or liver. Go to a quiet area with your dog, and hold the good treat behind your back. Show her the low value treat enclosed in your fist, but don't let her have it. You want her to be able to smell it, but not get it in her mouth. Say "Off" like a statement of fact (don't ask your dog a question here, or you might not like the answer!), and watch your dog like a hawk. Most dogs will sniff and smell your hand—some of them will even paw at it to get at the treat. Wait it out, ignoring all your dog's efforts to get at the treat. Eventually, sometimes within just a few seconds, your dog will take her attention off your fist, and either look up at you or in another direction. When she does, immediately praise and give her the high value treat from the *other hand.*

Repeat this exercise several times, always holding the low value treat in one hand and the high value one behind your back. In the early stages of training do NOT extend this to food or other treasures that your dog finds on the floor outside of a training session. That is a completely different context to your dog, and trying it now will compromise the foundation you are trying to build.

Aim for about two to five replicates in a session, being sure to end on a good note. Look for your dog to hesitate or back away from the food when hearing the word "off," without your having to block her. When she'll hesitate consistently, you're ready for the next step.

Food on the Floor Once your dog will pause when you have food in your hand, ask your dog to leave something alone that is on the ground. This is A LOT harder for your dog, so don't toss a treat on the ground, say "Off" and expect your dog to back away. She's been on a treasure hunt for food from the ground ever since she could walk, and she's not going to translate "Off" from food *in your hand* to food *on the ground* without your help.

Repeat the exercise as described above, by showing your dog the low value treat in one hand, saying "leave it" and giving her the extra good food from the other hand if she responds correctly. Once that has gone well at least twice, stand up and face your dog, and show her another low value treat. Say "leave it," but this time toss it a few feet behind you. Be sure that you give the verbal cue *before* you throw the treat, that's one of the details that's especially important. It's much harder for a dog to stop going forward once they're halfway there, so give her a chance to be right, and say "leave it," clearly and firmly before she's motivated to dash to the treat.

In an ideal world, the treat will have fallen two to three feet behind you and about a foot to the side. That location is best because it gives you the ability to Body Block her if she goes for the treat as soon as it falls. Most dogs will do exactly that, by the way, so be ready to move quickly between her and the treat. If you have to, step on the treat to prevent your dog from getting it. Some dogs will immediately defer, looking up at your face and even backing up a foot or two. If so, thank your lucky stars that you have such a wonderful dog, say "Good!" and give her the food from your other hand. Most dogs, however, have no intention of giving up that fast, so they counter your movement by trying to go around you. Your job is to keep your dog from getting the treat, so move left or right, doing whatever you need to do to block her from getting the treat, just as you'd try to block a soccer ball from going into the net. Meanwhile, watch for the slightest sign that your dog is hesitating, and is no longer trying to get the treat on the ground. Obvious signs are looking up at your face, backing up an inch or two, or walking away as if bored. However, some dogs will merely shift their bodies backward an inch or two. That's fine—you want to reinforce your dog for any action that tells you she's stopped trying to get at the treat, even if just for a moment. Once she'll pause on hearing the word "off" and doesn't need the body block as a reminder, begin to move further away from the food. (Do not do this without professional help if your dog might be aggressive to you over food!)

Teaching Off with More Than One Dog Once all of your dogs are reliable with "off," it is time to work on a group "off." Like the group "wait," begin with only two dogs. Say to your dogs, "Dogs, off," in a low-pitched voice. As this is a brand new context, they won't necessarily act as they do when they're alone. As before, be ready to block any forward motion toward the food. The instant that both dogs pause, say one of their names in your singsong "release" voice to release that dog. Only the dog whose name was called is permitted to come to the food and take it. Be prepared to body block the other dog. Repeat this right away and let the other dog have the food the next time so that each dog has a chance to be reinforced for being polite.

Refining Your Dogs' Patience in a Group Off When you practice group "offs," vary who gets the treat, and keep your dogs guessing who will get it next. As with the group "wait," you can decide who gets the treat by saying the name of the dog who does the best "off," although you want to mix it up so that every dog gets the treat sometimes.

A Group Off with the Whole Group Once you have worked with each possible pair of dogs in your household, begin trying it with all the threesomes. Say, "Dogs, off," and wait until all three dogs stay still or back away, not putting any pressure on you for the food. You may have to body block one or more dogs away from the food. Release one dog by saying his name cheerfully. Gradually increase the number of dogs until your whole brood is doing a lovely group off together. This may sound like a big project, but it is well worth it if you ever drop the Thanksgiving turkey onto the kitchen floor (we again speak from experience.)

Walking Multiple Dogs

Walking your dogs together can be the best of times, or the worst of them, so the subject deserves a little attention. It's one thing to let one dog pull you around the block, but it's another altogether to be hauled around by a team of dogs like a sled. Neighborhood walks with more than one dog have a way of illustrating how one dog's excitement can set off the whole group—nothing like having your beagle spot a rabbit to turn an evening stroll into an adventure. We can't suggest that reading a short booklet will turn your pack into the equivalent of synchronous swimmers, but we do have some ideas for you.

Good equipment: Don't leave home without it. You wouldn't dream of walking a group of draft horses down a busy street with inadequate equipment, so don't do it with your dogs. If you haven't noticed yet, 3 dogs pulling simultaneously in the same direction can generate enough force to pull a hay wagon, much less you and your over-powered body. Of course, that's nothing compared to having them pull in *different* directions! That's why you need to get physics on your side, and think about what equipment you use to walk your dogs.

Ideally, we could all walk our dogs on a buckle collar and a thin leash, (or better yet, no leash at all). But towns have leash laws and lots of dogs use buckle collars to throw their weight against the leash and pull like draft animals. You are much better off using a system that prevents rather than encourages pulling by your dogs. The device that works best for most dogs is called a "body harness." These harnesses differ from traditional harnesses because the leash attaches to a band that goes across your dog's chest, which prevents your dog from leaning forward and pushing against the chest band. Dogs accept these harnesses readily, and they almost miraculously decrease pulling. There are several brands on the market, including the original, the *SENSE-ation*™ *harness* by Softouch Concepts and the *Easy Walk harness* by Premier. If you don't have any of these body harnesses yet, and your dogs are hauling you around the neighborhood, put down this book and go get some. Remember, horse handlers don't feel guilty that they haven't trained a set of horses to walk 'on heel!' It's okay to find a humane, efficient method of controlling your dogs on a walk and use it without guilt. Besides, if you use the right equipment, your dog will have a better time too.

Another useful device is the "head collar," or *Gentle Leader*, which was the first effective and humane solution to walking a dog who was more interested in chasing a squirrel than walking beside you politely. Head collars look like the halters that horses wear, and allow you to control your dog's actions by controlling where his head is facing. When you pull on the leash, the dog's nose and his eyes are directed toward you. Dogs tend to think about what they're looking at, so once you have your dog looking at you, you're likely to have his attention as well. They are harder for some dogs to get used to, but can be a wonderful helper for extra-large and extra-exuberant dogs whose owners need as much physics on their side as they can get.

We aren't in favor of the old fashioned way of preventing pulling, by using "choke" collars that tighten continually the harder the dog pulls, or "prong" collars with spikes that press into the dog's neck. Both of these methods can work for some people, but more often they either hurt or scare the dog, or just simply don't work. Choke collars are especially ineffective for many dogs, who are amazingly resistant to increasing levels of pressure around their necks (as anyone who has listened to their dog gagging down the street knows), and prong collars can hurt dogs and/or elicit defensive aggression. Body harnesses and head collars are effective and humane, so don't hesitate to give them a try.

One last word of advice: you'd be smart to get one dog at a time used to wearing anything new, and you used to using it, before you hitch up the entire team. Body harnesses don't really take any training on your part, but you'd be wise to get used to the feel of them before you venture out the door with your brood. Head collars need to be fitted correctly, so read the instructions carefully before using them or get professional help to be sure it fits just right.

One at a Time. We've had lots of clients who had nothing but trouble trying to walk their two or three dogs around the neighborhood. Perhaps one dog was reactive to other dogs and set the rest of the group off into a maelstrom of barking and leaping. In some cases one dog would re-direct to his housemate, and start nipping and barking at him instead of another dog who was barking from behind a fence in a neighbor's backyard. In either case the hapless human stood in the middle of a tsunami of dogs, usually pondering the benefits of cat ownership.

All of these clients were grateful when we said: "You know, it's okay to not walk all your dogs at the same time." That may seem like a stunningly obvious thing to say, but when you're the one in the middle of a forest of paws, it's easy to lose track of the path out of the woods. We are all so conditioned to believe that all of our dogs need to be taken on a walk, that sometimes it's hard to justify leaving a dog behind. We're here to say "Hey, it's okay. It might even be better." Strolling around a neighborhood may seem like the simplest thing in the world to us, but it actually can be difficult for a dog. Dogs on leash have no social freedom, and sidewalks force them to walk in unnaturally straight lines. Direct head-on approaches are horribly rude in dog societies, a fact we often forget as we walk toward another set of dog walkers coming toward us on a narrow sidewalk.

If one of your dogs has issues during neighborhood walks, you'd be wise to either walk him by himself or find other ways for him to exercise and relieve himself. Walking a dog by himself has many benefits—you can concentrate on helping him through his "issues," what ever they may be (if he's dog-dog reactive, see our *Feisty Fido* booklet), or you could just let him enjoy having your full attention. Walks are a great time to get one-on-one time with each dog, so think about taking one dog on his own "special" walk when you can.

Of course, separate walks take lots more time, and you simply may not have it. That might not be a problem—in some cases your dog might be better off skipping neighborhood walks while you work on building a foundation of behaviors to help him respond appropriately to other dogs or unfamiliar people. You can use trick training and exercises inside the house and yard to keep the non-walker busy and in condition.

Be proactive. Neighborhood walks are a great time to both practice and use the cues we've introduced earlier. Say one of your dogs sees a squirrel up ahead. Your other dog hasn't seen it yet, and he's the one who goes insane every time he sees the furry little tease. "Dogs, Wait!" you say in a clear, low pitched voice. If your dogs have learned the "wait" cue, they will all pause, giving you a chance to turn around and stride off in the other direction. This is also a handy cue to use if another group of dogs approaches—take your dogs off to the side and say "Wait." Be ready with lots of praise and treats as your dogs sit quietly (and give yourself some chocolate!).

On the other hand, perhaps you spot a filthy food wrapper in the gutter, and you know one of your dogs can be aggressively possessive over such treasures. "Dog, Off!" you say, before trouble can start. Of course, when the dogs pause you give them lots of reinforcement and move away in another direction.

Don't forget that you have to practice these exercises in the context of walks—they won't work if you've only done them in the living room. This is another reason to go out of your way to walk only one dog at a time on occasion. Walks are a great opportunity to work with one dog at a time when there are a lot of distractions competing for his attention. Remember that it's much harder for him to listen and respond when the breeze is blowing and the kids are playing soccer across the street. You'll need to be ready with lots of great reinforcements, and a clear understanding that his skills are going to degrade a bit from what they were inside the house. Expect his skills to falter a bit the first time you say "wait" when you're outside, and be ready to have a party when he gets it right.

Teach polite walking to each dog, one at a time.

Dogs don't come hard-wired to walk side-by-side with us, and the problem is compounded when we take a group of them out together. Sometimes you can solve all your problems by using the right equipment, as we discussed above, but it never hurts to teach your dogs that humans play a silly game called "walk side-by-side with me, and ignore everything else that is interesting." If you reinforce your dog correctly for it, he'll decide that silly as it is, it's worth it to walk like a human instead of a dog. (Well, okay, not on two legs, but you get the idea.)

Take it from us, things will go much more smoothly if you start with one dog at a time. We haven't met a trainer yet who can reinforce three dogs effectively at the same time, so spend a little time with each dog before you put everybody back together as a group, Teaching polite leash-walking is described in detail in *Family Friendly Dog Training*, but we'll summarize here so you can get started.

Step One Start by teaching your dog that it's fun to stay with you as you walk. Go outside to a relatively quiet area, and show your dog that you have extra tasty treats in your left hand. Once he's starting to drool, stride forward away from your dog, with your dog on your left hand side. You goal is to reinforce your dog for keeping up with you, so do whatever you need to do to keep him beside you. You can slap your left leg, smooch or make clicking noises, speed up as if to run away, and/or wave the treat down by your left knee. If your dog has stayed up with you after two or three strides, even if he's a bit behind you, give him praise and a treat, making sure to treat him while he's standing beside you. Don't make him come in front of you to get the treat, you want him to learn it's fun to stand alongside. If he hasn't been keeping up with you, go back to him and put the treat within an inch of his nose. If he ignores it and goes back to sniffing the grass, go back inside and get a better treat! (Some dogs might do better with a tennis ball or squeaky toy.) If he gets ahead of you, just turn and go the other way, and give him a treat when he catches back up to you.

Your goal is to be so interesting that your dog can't help but want to walk beside you. One of the ways to do that is to vary your direction and speed—most of us walk too slowly to be interesting to our dogs, so speed up for a stride or two and see if that keeps your dog's attention. Try this a couple of times a day, for very short periods of time, no more than a minute or two at first. As usual, only try this when there are few distractions and you are sure that your dog is hungry for the goodies you've got in your pocket.

Step Two Once this is going well, try something a little different. Rather than "helping" your dog catch up with you, remain silent and walk in big circles around your dog. The idea is to teach your dog that it's fun to pay attention to you, and that wonderful things happen if he decides *on his own* to join up and walk beside you. Don't do anything to try to get your dog to follow you, just walk away. Your job is to walk in big circles around your dog, perhaps ten to fifteen feet away, waiting for that magic moment when he decides to catch up with you. Resist the urge to lure your dog with the treat, to call, clap or, for that matter, to pay any attention to your dog whatsoever. You can do this on a loose leash or better yet, in a safe, fenced area where you can drop the leash and try it with no physical connection to your dog.

33

This is not easy for most of us! It's hard to walk away without trying to 'help' your dog, but stay focused on walking purposefully by yourself; this game is all about your dog making his own decision, not about you helping him to do the right thing. We want him to learn there's a good reason to choose you over everything else in the environment, so do your best to ignore him completely as you stride around him as if you were late for a meeting.

Watch him out of the corner of your eye, and the instant he approaches within a foot or so, stop walking and give him lots of praise and several wonderful treats. Now try walking away again, watching for the next time he moves toward you. As soon as it feels like he's "caught up," treat him again, and then resume walking.

Step Three Once your dog starts learning that wonderful things happen if he catches up to you, start walking with him on a leash as if you were taking a neighborhood walk. Continue to give him a treat every time he catches up to you, and give him extra treats if you stays with you as you move forward. This is a good time to put his behavior on cue: say "Heel" every time you move forward when he is by your side. Give him lots of treats with your left hand (try not to turn your body toward him, that will just act like a body block and stop his forward motion). If he takes off away from you after he gets his treat, simply stop and wait for him to look or move toward you. Praise him the moment that he does, even if all he does is turn his head. Once he moves into heel position, shower him with treats and move forward energetically to keep his attention. If he gets ahead of you, turn and go the other way, and give him treats as soon as he gets in heel position. Remember that heel requires your dog to concentrate on you above all else, so reciprocate by staying focused on him while he's learning to heel. Be sure to release him from his heel clearly; think of heel as something like a "walking stay," and make it clear to him when he can change his focus and be released from your heel cue.

In the early stages, give him *lots* of reinforcement if he stays up with you. Remember—heeling isn't natural to dogs, and it goes against their instincts. Your job is to be the most interesting game in town, and you've got a lot of competition out there. The most common mistake that beginners make is not giving their dogs enough treats in the early stages of heel training, so be generous!

Gradually increase the time period between treats, asking your dog to stay up with you for three strides, then five, etc. etc. Intersperse short sessions of heeling with long walks during which your equipment keeps your dog from pulling, and you'll find your dog gets better and better at heeling when you need it.

Step Four Of course, the last step is to put your dogs together and work on this as a group. You will probably find that dogs who were great on their own have a lot more trouble walking politely when there's another dog beside them. Some dogs seem be wired like racehorses, and hate it when another dog gets ahead of them. Others will want to lag behind, and you'll have to encourage them to catch up. Some people find their dogs do best if they all walk on one side, while others like one dog on one side, and one or more on the other. No one can tell you what is best for you and your dogs, but we do suggest that you be observant and sensitive to what your dogs are telling you—some dogs aren't comfortable walking beside a particular dog. If one of your dogs is avoiding walking side-by-side with another, honor that preference and work it out another way. We suspect that lots of fights are caused by owners forcing dogs into interacting in ways that they were desperately trying to avoid.

Play

One of the advantages of having multiple dogs is that they always have someone to play with. They get the exercise and fun of play, while you get to hang out with a cup of coffee on the porch. But sometimes canine play can get pretty, uh…exuberant. When your dogs are rolling around like some cartoon tumbleweed of rotating teeth, paws, and tails, it's natural to wonder if everyone is going to survive. It's good to be concerned that your dogs play in a safe, acceptable way, because just like sporting events, play can be so exciting that sometimes it gets out of hand. But how can you tell what's just boisterous fun and what is play that leads to trouble? Although there is a lot of variation in how dogs play, there are some specific behaviors you can observe in your dogs to help you figure out if they are having good, wholesome fun, or starting to spiral toward a brawl. In appropriate play, all dogs are willing participants. There is usually much chasing of one another, delightful frolics in circles and lots of rolling on the ground together; sometimes with periodic play bows to keep things going. Often when they're engaged in "rough and tumble" play and one dog is on his back and the other is standing, the dogs will switch places, alternating who is on top. All the dogs engaged in a healthy play bout are willing participants, so if you're not sure if their play is still really "playful," you can always gently separate them and see if they all choose to go back for more. If one dog slinks away, then you know that the play session was getting out of hand.

A lot of dog owners worry about the fact that their dogs use their teeth and mouths so much, but that's a normal part of play in canids. Dogie play bouts are similar in one way to the wrestle play of children, where each participant tries to gain a physical advantage over the other. The primary difference is that in dogs, the players are trying to "play bite" each other more than wrestle the other down to the ground. A well-matched group of dogs tends to play with their mouths open a lot, and show inhibited play bites directed toward the legs and paws of other dogs. But even though they look like they're trying to bite each other, their bites are inhibited and their mouths don't stay attached in the same place for more than a few seconds. Your dogs are likely to use their paws a lot, too, pawing and batting, without enough force to hurt each other.

But sometimes play can spiral into a fight, and even if it doesn't, sometimes one dog might be having a good time while another dog is not. Healthy play in dogs can be so noisy and look so out-of-control that it's hard to know if the dogs are playing or working their way up into a fight. Because much of play in dogs is really "play fights," it's not always easy to tell which is which. Inappropriate play can take on many forms, but it almost always results in one or more dogs becoming frightened, hurt, or overwhelmed. There are some things that you can watch out for that can help alert you to possible problems. First of all, if one dog is always on top and the dog on the bottom is trying to get out from under, or if there is one dog who tries repeatedly to get away and hide under furniture, then the play is likely not appropriate. Just like on a playground, it's possible for some dogs to be having fun at the expense of others.

Another aspect of play to monitor is the way that your dogs mouth each other in play. Play bites are a natural part of play, but if much of the mouthing consists of hard bites to a playmate, the play is too rough. Play bites shouldn't last for longer than a few seconds. Often if one dog gets too rough, and isn't inhibiting his bites well enough, you'll hear yelps from the other dogs. If one dog starts yelping, he is probably scared or in pain, and that's a clear sign to intervene. (The occasional brief yelp may just mean there was an accidental collision of some kind, the dog equivalent of stepping on your partner's toes while dancing. The other dog should then stop immediately in acknowledgement of his partner's "ouch.")

You are also wise to listen for escalating growls during a play bout. Play is arousing and emotionally exciting, and dogs can sometimes start play with all the best of intentions and then inadvertently spiral themselves up into aggression. Sporting events are famous for this progression, as in the expression "I went to a fight and a hockey game broke out." So listen to your dogs while they're playing. Typical play growls can sound quite intense, and aren't anything to worry about. But if they start to get louder and lower pitched, then you'd be wise to redirect your dogs to another activity for awhile. The key is to listen for an escalation of intensity.

Another possible sign of impending trouble is if your dogs consistently play up on their hind legs for more than a few seconds. If this goes on for a long period, and their growls start escalating, then you may have dogs who are taking play a bit too seriously, and trying to work out some conflict through play. Other signs to watch for that lead to problems are the relentless mounting, clasping, and thrusting onto one dog by another. Dogs who constantly try to lay their paws, heads or their whole bodies across the shoulders of another dog may be trying to achieve social status or simply intimidate the other dog, so this behavior should be carefully monitored and redirected if it occurs consistently. Pouncing on another dog in a cat-like way is another common type of play that is acceptable depending on its frequency and intensity. If it's relentless and the "victim" dog tries to get away, then by all means, interrupt the session.

Even if your dogs are playing appropriately, it's possible for too much of a good thing to lead to trouble. While it's good for your dogs (and your soul) for them to play together, sometimes it is good to separate your dogs and have them take a break. There are several motivations for limiting or interrupting your dogs' play with each other. First, it's not good for your dogs to play constantly with each other, spending most of their day out on the playground with their buddies. If they do, you become the odd one out, the boring old parent who does nothing but impose rules and regulations. If their best friends are each other, and all of their best times are dog-only situations, where does that leave you? Second, excessive play can get dogs overly excited and that arousal can lead dogs from play fighting to actual fighting. Your dogs need breaks, even from too much fun with each other, so they don't get overly aroused.

Third, it's perfectly reasonable to interrupt your dogs' play because it is giving you a headache or you can't hear the television! You don't have to put up with play that is noisy and bothersome just because your dogs are having a good time. Compromise is essential when you share a home with others, no matter what the species. Your dogs should get to make a bit of a racket sometimes, but you don't have to resign yourself to tolerating it constantly. Go ahead and separate your dogs when you want to. Put them in different areas of the house, give them chew toys to keep them occupied, or put them on down-stays. It's good for them to take a break, and it's good for you to take care of yourself. Later, when you're in the mood to appreciate their zaniness, and they've had chance to calm down, let them play some more.

STAYING AWAY FROM TROUBLE

Prevention

Prevention is a powerful, active training tool and not a cop out. If you are working on correcting a situation among your dogs such as dinnertime scuffles or frenzied greetings when visitors come to the door, prevention should be part of your plan. It's not "giving up" to feed your dogs separately, or to let only one go to the door when the bell rings until your dogs can be polite as a group. If you are unsure about what might happen in a particular context, it's okay to avoid the situation until you're sure how to handle it. Don't put yourself in the "hope-and-fear" zone ("I hope it's going to be okay, but I fear that it won't be!") The "hope-and-fear" zone is not a fun place to be. Some temporary preventive tools you can try are feeding dogs separately, walking dogs separately or at less crowded times of day, crating one or more dogs while you are away, using gates to separate your dogs, and removing the objects that cause conflict such as bones, rawhides, or balls.

Thank You for Not Fighting or Making Threats in Our Home

Your dogs should learn that they will not get what they want if they make threats or fight. In most households an occasional growl or tooth display is not a crisis. But if there's continual unresolved tension between two dogs, be conservative and intervene long before an actual fight occurs. Respond to a snarl or lunge quickly and definitively. Whenever two dogs have "issues" with one another, any type of threat whether it's a growl, a snap, or an aggressive visual display is an "incident" and a fight is just an incident that has been allowed to escalate out of control. If things start to escalate, don't start screaming and yelling. If you're like most of us, you might have to hold your hand over your mouth to stay quiet, but do whatever it takes to keep yourself quiet. If a calm low-pitched "No!" or "Hey!" doesn't stop the aggression (or threat of it), then getting louder probably won't either. In fact, yelling often adds to the drama and in most cases makes things worse. A distraction such as saying "Let's go for a walk," or putting both dogs into a long down-stay is more apt to stop trouble than yelling.

If your dogs actually get into a fight, the first thing to do is to separate the dogs to keep them safe. Depending on the seriousness of the fight, this may involve body blocking or calling your dogs away from each other, making a loud startling noise to interrupt them, or physically pulling them apart. There's no completely safe way to separate dogs in a fight, so be aware that you might get hurt if you try to pull two dogs apart. Avoid reaching in and pulling dogs apart by their collars if you can. When they are excited, many dogs will turn their mouths on you if they are grabbed by the collar. It is best to pull dogs apart by their back legs or tails, but of course this takes two people if the dogs are relatively large. To keep your body out of the way of those teeth, you can also try the famous water hose technique (it does work sometimes), spray citronella at them or in desperation, use a fire extinguisher. One of our clients tossed her two fighting dogs into the pool. It worked beautifully, but might be a bit expensive if you don't have one already.

Once the dogs are safely separated, assume a stern but quiet manner, communicating to your dogs that you are calm (even if you're not!) and in control. Again, remember that yelling just adds to the excitement. Stand between the scrappers and put them in down-stays as far away from each other as you can while they are still in sight of each other. Don't do this if there's a danger that one will break a stay and resume the hostilities. The down-stay should last anywhere from a few minutes to half an hour, depending on what your dogs are capable of maintaining. The down-stay provides a cooling-off period without rewarding any of the dogs. If one dog is taken out of the room the other dog may perceive that she "won"—after all, she finally got rid of that miserable cur, even if just for a short while! When you release your dogs from their stays, ignore them, separating them for safety if you need to by putting them in different rooms or in their crates. If you can't use down-stays, separate the dogs with gates or crates, but if possible keep them in sight of one another.

How long you ignore them depends on the seriousness of the fight. For a mild transgression, you might ignore them for half an hour, but for a serious fight, ignoring them for a whole day is not unreasonable. That means being in the same room with your dogs but actively refusing to acknowledge their existence, not confining them away from you. If separating the dogs for safety's sake means that they must be in different places, go to the one whose behavior you consider most unacceptable and proceed with another down-stay. Don't praise your dogs for this down-stay. Dogs who have just fought or made threats to another dog don't need to hear the voice of approval when you are rightfully disgusted with the behavior you've just witnessed. If there is more than one person at home at the time of the incident, a different person can attend to each dog.

At one time or another you have probably been advised to "let your dogs work it out." But your dogs will learn more (and it is much less risky), if you take charge of the situation and stop unacceptable behavior. Just as teachers and parents step in to stop arguments, we prefer to stop an incident before it escalates. There are two reasons for this: One, if the incidents are stopped, your dogs will learn that fighting does not get them what they want. It's too easy for one dog to "win" in a fight and learn that fighting is a successful strategy. Two, fights can and do result in serious injuries and even death. Don't take that chance. Even if injuries are minor and heal quickly, it is devastating to watch two animals you love hurt each other. Don't feel badly about successfully stopping a fight. Instead, congratulate yourself.

Often, dogs are relieved, not distressed, that a fight has been stopped. After all, aren't some guys grateful to their buddies when they physically restrain them from clobbering some loud mouth in a bar? They don't lose face, but they don't have to fight either.

COMING AND GOING

So You Want Another Dog?

It was the best of plans, it was the worst of plans. Adding another dog to your house can multiply the charms and joys of dog ownership. However, adding a dog to your household can also magnify the dark side of dog behavior and lead to canine jealousies, impatience, frustration, lack of sleep (for you), and even fighting.

If you are considering adding another dog to your life and to your home, base your decision on whether this addition is in the best interests of everyone: you, your dogs, the new dog, and your human family. As understandable as it is, please don't base your decision on having lost your heart to a dog that needs a home or the desire to get a dog who looks exactly like the one whose loss you are still grieving. It is so often tempting to add "just one more" to the pack, but all of us have our limits, as do our dogs. Adding "just one more" creates havoc too many times in what had been a mellow household, so think carefully before you lose your heart. If you are thinking of getting another dog, ask yourself the following questions:

- How do my dogs get along with each other right now?

- How do my dogs get along with new dogs that they meet? In my yard? In my house?

- Does the dog I am considering get along well with other dogs?

- Do I have the time to devote to integrating a new dog into the group?

- Do I have the time to establish a relationship with the new dog by having just the two of us spend time together?

44

- Do I have the physical set up at home to temporarily separate dogs at first?

- Do all family members agree that getting a new dog is a good idea?

- Will getting another dog add an unmanageable financial burden?

- What will I do if it does not work out?

- Do I want my spouse or partner to go crazy?

Introducing New Dogs to Each Other

To get off on the right paw with a new dog, it helps to be thoughtful about their introduction. Your dog(s) and the new dog are about to have the equivalent of a blind date and arranged marriage (Hi! Nice to meet you. Now let's live together...) You will want to do what you can to make sure the atmosphere is just right and that first impressions are as favorable as possible.

First, learn what you can about the new dog's history with other dogs. If your dog and the new dog are both dog-social and laid back when meeting other dogs, the odds are in your favor that the introduction will go smoothly. If one of them gets scared or obnoxious when meeting new dogs, you will obviously want to take that into account and proceed more slowly and cautiously. Let one dog at a time meet the new dog so that the newcomer is not overwhelmed by your whole crew at once.

For your best shot at a friendly, successful introduction, have the dogs meet "off-territory" rather than at your house or in your yard. A neutral area such as a neighbor's yard, a training center, or a tennis court works best. Ideally, the dogs can get a chance to look at each other and sniff each other through a barrier such as a fence or gate for as little as 30 seconds or as long as 30 minutes. By the time the dogs are ready to interact without barriers, the novelty of the new dog has worn off and the introduction has a better chance of being a positive experience for both dogs.

Another way to let the novelty wear off prior to any interaction is to take the dogs on a walk together. It's best in some cases to initially keep the dogs far enough apart that they can't greet. Walk them in the same direction, avoiding having them stare at each other and keep them at a distance of at least ten feet from each other when you begin.

Once they're ready, let the dogs greet one another off leash. Being leashed makes many dogs more tense. (If "fight" and "flight" are the two primary responses to feeling insecure in a new situation, and the leash takes away the flight option, guess what's left?) So, for safety, a large fenced-in area is ideal. If no such safe area is available to you, and you must introduce your dogs on leashes, at least avoid having the leashes be tight. All that tension to a dog's collar and neck sets the wrong tone. What you want is a happy, relaxed, carefree meeting, not "Boy are things tense around here!"

In selecting an area for the introduction, avoid loaded areas such as gates or doorways, or any closely confined space. The more the dogs are free to move around, the more likely they are to have a positive experience. In thinking about this goal of open space, be conscious of how the people present can affect the space available to the dogs. Avoid clustering people around the dogs in a tight, tense circle, and be careful to give the dogs room to move. As the dogs begin to sniff each other, call them away and move around for a minute or two. By moving away from the dogs, you can draw away any tension and keep the mood relaxed and light. If they start to play right away and it all just seems perfect, let them play for a few minutes and then end the session. You want to end on a good note and leave them wanting more of each other.

Don't risk having their new relationship go south by letting the first meeting go on and on until something bad happens.

If you have reason to suspect trouble, or just don't know what to expect, your best strategy, as radical as it may sound, is to condition both dogs to muzzles and to use them when they first meet. In addition to making injuries less likely, the muzzles can give you more confidence so you can do your part to remain calm and relaxed and not let your tension infect your dogs' first encounter with each other.

Once the dogs have met off-territory, the next step is to have them meet at your home. First have them meet in your yard if possible, especially if it is fenced. The next step is to have them meet in your house. Begin by taking the resident dogs out and letting the new dog in first. Having a new dog enter a house with a resident dog in it is potentially a high-arousal situation. It is more likely to lead to trouble to have a new dog enter than to have your resident dogs come into their house to find a new dog already there. Keep these early meetings short (less than a few minutes) so that the dogs do not get tired out by their new social demands.

Please view these guidelines for introducing new dogs as a general plan. As with anything, there will be exceptions. If you expect problems when introducing a new dog or if you think it would be best to introduce your dogs in a different way, please seek out a professional to help you with the introduction. The first meeting can set the tone of the relationship to follow, so do everything you can to make the initial meeting as successful as possible.

While their relationship is still new, be conservative about when your new dog is left alone with the others. Don't let all your dogs be together when you first leave them alone. Separate them with gates or put them in different rooms or in crates. Start off right away with all the exercises we discuss in this booklet, including "Being Comfortable Alone." Getting off to the right start immediately can do wonders in creating the harmony you desire (and deserve). If your new dog's prior life has been a difficult one of neglect and abuse, resist the temptation to cater shamelessly to him. It won't make his painful past go away, but it might compromise his future.

Signs That May Indicate A Serious Problem

This booklet was written to help you enjoy your group of dogs even more, and to help decrease tension that may exist or develop between your dogs. If your problems with your dogs involve more serious aggression, this booklet can still help, but we encourage you to consult privately with a qualified trainer or behaviorist. Here is a list of signs that may indicate serious problems between your dogs.

Not all of the things listed below necessarily mean that your dogs are dealing with an aggression issue. For example, lots of us have dogs that are a bit jealous of the attention given to another dog. Don't panic if your dogs show a couple of the milder symptoms, but do watch out for these signs and note any signs of increasing tension.

- One dog consistently pushes others aside for access to your petting and attention.

- Your dogs guard their food bowls from one another.

- Your dogs are frequently up on their back paws during play.

- One dog seems "jealous" of the attention you give to another dog.

- Your dogs always seem to watch each other warily.

- One dog protects you (like a bone) from the other dogs.

- "Dirty looks" (hard stares and glares) are passing between two or more of your dogs.

- You find yourself tense and anxious about what might happen between your dogs.

- Your dogs exhibit stiff postures around each other.

- One dog bullies the other dogs, taking away all their bones and toys.

- One of your dogs keeps another dog from moving freely around the house.

- One of your dogs slinks around the house, avoiding another dog.

- Your dogs growl, snap, show their teeth, or lunge at each other.

- And, of course, your dogs are fighting with each other.

Rehoming

One of the most difficult behavior problems to treat involves dogs in a household who act as though they despise one another. In some cases, the dogs are willing to severely injure each other, and even risk their own lives to eliminate their rival. This is most often true of warring females. Since a harassed dog can't strike out on her own if she needs to, sometimes the best thing you can do for her (or him) is to find one of your dogs a new home. This can be very hard on us, but it is important to consider the quality of life of each individual animal living in your home.

While the humans in the household may experience each and every dog as a loving, caring, integral part of the family, your dogs may be having a very different experience. The dog that you see as kind and affectionate may be experienced by another dog as a dangerous bully. If one of your dogs slinks around the house, avoids any area of the house, and is constantly on guard and aware of where another dog is, then this dog's quality of life isn't very good.

We know that it's easy to be overwhelmed by guilt when you think about rehoming a dog, feeling like you are betraying a best friend or family member. But think about the responsibility you took on when you first got the dog. Responsible owners agree to look out for the best interests of the pets they have and to do what they can to give them the very best life possible. Sometimes, this "best life" might not be with you. Your house and your family of pets may make your otherwise wonderful home a great place for some dogs, but not for others. If this is the case, placing a dog you cherish in another home may be the most responsible, as well as the most humane and loving, thing you can do for your dog. Taking on a lifelong obligation to an animal sometimes means considering the possibility that your home, through no fault whatsoever of yours, may not be the ideal environment for this particular dog. One of us has rehomed several dogs and between us we've now owned three rehomed ones, so our support of rehoming dogs under certain circumstances is very real and very personal.

CONCLUSION

You don't need us to tell you that: (1) It can be wonderful to have more than one dog and (2) It can be incredibly challenging to have more than one dog. Our hope is that the advice in this booklet, developed from years of helping clients to manage their multi-dog households, will help the "wonderful" outweigh the "challenging." May you experience all the joys of living with all your dogs, and never feel outnumbered again.

Still Feeling Outnumbered?

Patricia B. McConnell, PhD

Feeling Outnumbered?
How to manage and enjoy
your multi-dog household

PMC

Don't miss the *Feeling Outnumbered?* DVD that accompanies this booklet! It provides exercises clearly illustrated by Patricia in her own home, and will help anyone who wouldn't mind living with a little less canine commotion.

"I recently purchased the Feeling Outnumbered? book and DVD. I have read many books and watched many DVDs on dog training, and this set is one of the best for people with multiple dogs in their home. It has helped me and my family with our three dogs, and I would highly recommend this book and DVD to anyone who has more than one dog." Frank R. Elmsford, NY

Running Time: 1hr 45min

Who Should Buy This DVD?

Dog Owners

As everyone with multiple dogs knows, having two dogs can be more than twice the fun (and work) of one. This DVD will show you how to manage your pack, by teaching them to get what they want by being polite rather than pushy.

Trainers, Behaviorists, Veterinarians & Veterinary Technicians

This is one of the few resources available that addresses the unique demands of a multi-dog household. Let it help you assist your clients when the situation gets "out of hand" (paw?).

Rescues/Foster Homes

Busy foster homes can use some of the techniques in Feeling Outnumbered? to help them manage their ever-changing group of dogs. The sections on introducing new dogs and reading signs of potential aggression are especially useful for people bringing fosters into their homes.

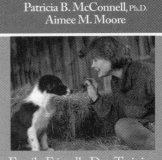
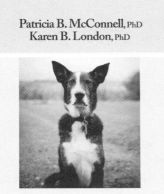

PATRICIA
McCONNELL, PH.D.
Your source for science and soul in dog training and behavior

www.patriciamcconnell.com/store

Patricia's books, booklets, and DVDs are used by thousands of professionals all over the world because they are clear, user-friendly and employ positive dog training methods. Topics range from teaching a dog to come when called and walking politely on a leash, to treating serious behavior problems such as aggression or separation anxiety. Special pricing is available for bulk purchases.

www.patriciamcconnell.com/learning-center

Walk right in, get comfy and savor a comprehensive compilation of Patricia's articles, blog posts, and videos about dogs and the people who love them.

www.theeducationofwill.com

Interweaving enlightening stories of her clients' dogs with tales of her deepening bond with Will, Patricia describes her efforts to recover from her traumatic past. Hopeful and inspiring, the redemptive message of her journey reminds us that, "while trauma changes our brains, and the past casts a long shadow, healing for both people and dogs is possible through hard work, compassion, and mutual devotion".

Follow Patricia on Social Media

https://twitter.com/mcconnellwrites
https://www.facebook.com/PatriciaMcConnellPhD
https://www.youtube.com/user/PatriciaMcConnell

Join the Pack!

Sign up for our email list and we'll send you a
Coupon Code for 10% Off your next order!

Email support@patriciamcconnell.com with the subject:
Feeling Outnumbered Coupon Code

Receive updates about products, events and special promotions in our newsletters. Stay informed about new research on canine and feline behavior, not to mention the world's most complicated animals (us!). You will also receive information on upcoming events, and anything else our dogs and cats encourage us to add. To ensure you receive our newsletter, add info@patriciamcconnell.com to your email address book.

Rest assured, your privacy is of utmost importance to us. We will never sell, borrow, or give away your information. You can leave the pack at anytime by replying to the email with "UNSUBSCRIBE" in the subject line.

Patricia McConnell, Ph.D. is an Ethologist and Certified Applied Animal Behaviorist who has consulted with cat and dog lovers for over twenty years. She combines a thorough understanding of the science of behavior with years of practical, applied experience. Her nationally syndicated radio show, Wisconsin Public Radio's *Calling All Pets,* plays in over 115 cities. She was the behavior columnist for The Bark magazine ("the New Yorker of Dog Magazines") and a Consulting Editor for the Journal of Comparative Psychology. She is Adjunct Associate Professor in Zoology at the University of Wisconsin-Madison, teaching "The Biology and Philosophy of Human/Animal Relationships." Dr. McConnell is a much sought after speaker and seminar presenter, speaking to training organizations, veterinary conferences, academic meetings and animal shelters around the world about dog and cat behavior, and on science-based and humane solutions to serious behavioral problems. She is the author of numerous books on training and behavioral problems, as well as the critically acclaimed books *The Other End of the Leash: Why We Do What We Do Around Dogs* and *For the Love of a Dog: Understanding Emotion in You and Your Best Friend.* For more information, go to www.patriciamcconnell.com and catch up with Patricia on her blog at www.theotherendoftheleash.com.

Karen B. London, Ph.D. received her B.S. in Biology from UCLA and her Doctorate in Zoology from the University of Wisconsin. Her research and scholarly publications cover such diverse topics as interactions between species that live together, defensive and aggressive behavior, evolution of social behavior, communication within and between species, learning, and parental investment. Dr. London is a Certified Applied Animal Behaviorist and a Certified Pet Dog Trainer whose clinical work focuses on the evaluation and treatment of serious behavioral problems in dogs. Karen London is currently a columnist for The Bark Magazine and served for three years on the Animal Behavior Society's Board of Professional Certification. She has written widely about training and behavior as well as giving educational seminars and speeches on canine behavior for trainers, veterinary and shelter staff, and the public. She is a lecturer at Northern Arizona University for a tropical biology field course to Nicaragua, and has given guest lectures in Animal Behavior at several universities. She lives in Flagstaff, Arizona with her husband and their two young sons. Visit Karen on her blog at www.dogbehaviorblog.com.